# Lightning

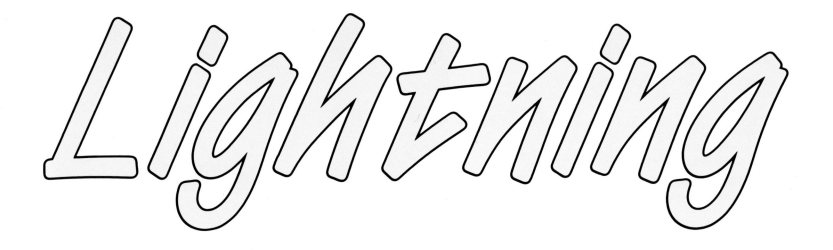

# by Stephen Kramer
# photographs by Warren Faidley

NATURE IN ACTION

Carolrhoda Books, Inc./Minneapolis

Additional photographs courtesy of: Japanese Information Center of Ball Lightning, photographer Y. Ouchi, p. 41; National Aeronautics and Space Administration, photographer Sam Walton, p. 46. The photographs of lightning sensors, on page 17, were taken through the permission of Lightning Location and Protection, Inc. David J. Firestine, Vice President of Operations, was generous enough to be photographed with his company's sensor equipment.

*This book is available in two editions:*
Library binding by Carolrhoda Books, Inc.,
  a division of Lerner Publishing Group
Soft cover by First Avenue Editions,
  an imprint of Lerner Publishing Group
241 First Avenue North
Minneapolis, MN 55401 U.S.A.

Website address: www.lernerbooks.com

Library of Congress Cataloging-in-Publication Data

Kramer, Stephen P.
  Lightning / by Stephen Kramer; photographs by Warren Faidley.
      p.  cm.  — (Nature in Action)
  Summary: Covers a variety of facts on lightning, including how it is formed, the different types of lightning, what thunder is and its relationship to lightning, safety measures, etc.
    ISBN-13: 978-0-87614-659-0 (lib. bdg. : alk. paper)
    ISBN-10: 0-87614-659-0 (lib. bdg. : alk. paper)
    ISBN-13: 978-0-87614-617-0 (pbk. : alk. paper)
    ISBN-10: 0-87614-617-5 (pbk. : alk. paper)
    1. Lightning—Juvenile literature.  [1. Lightning.]
I. Faidley, Warren, ill.  II. Title.  III. Series.
QC966.5.K73  1991
551.5'632—dc20                                          91-21793

Manufactured in the United States of America
10 11 12 13 14 15 – JR – 10 09 08 07 06 05

*For Jim and Pat*

With thanks to Dr. Martin A. Uman, an expert in lightning research at the University of Florida, and Dr. Robert Nemzek, from the Physics Department at the University of Minnesota, for their assistance with this book.

Much of the information explained in this book is based on the writings of Dr. Martin A. Uman. If you would like to know more about lightning, read the following book by Dr. Uman:

*All About Lightning.*
New York: Dover, 1986.

# Contents

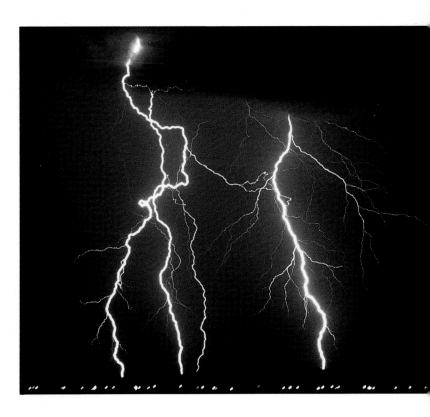

Late in the evening, a dark cloud hangs in the sky. The air is calm. The birds are quiet. Even the blades of dry grass are still. Everything is hushed, waiting.

6

Suddenly a giant spark leaps through the air, connecting earth and sky. The spark flickers for an instant and disappears. There is a moment of silence. Then a tremendous CRACK rips through the quiet. Booming echoes follow, rolling across the land.

A thunderstorm drifts across the summer sky.

At any moment, there are about 1,800 thunderstorms happening around the world. About 100 lightning bolts strike the earth every second.

Lightning is one of the most powerful forces of nature. It sets off raging forest fires. It destroys buildings. It kills plants, animals, and people. But it also balances out the natural electricity of the earth and sky.

For people living long ago, lightning was a great mystery. No one knew why lightning bolts shot through the air. No one understood how lightning made the dark clouds rumble. People told stories about gods or magical animals to explain what they saw and heard.

Even today, many things about lightning are still a mystery. But scientists are learning more and more about what happens when a flash of lightning streaks across the sky.

# What Is Lightning?

Lightning is a very large electrical spark. The spark is caused by tiny particles, called electrons, moving suddenly from one place to another.

Electrons are much too small to see. However, during a lightning flash, electrons shoot through the air so fast they make the air around them glow. A streak of lightning shows the path the electrons followed as they blasted their way forward.

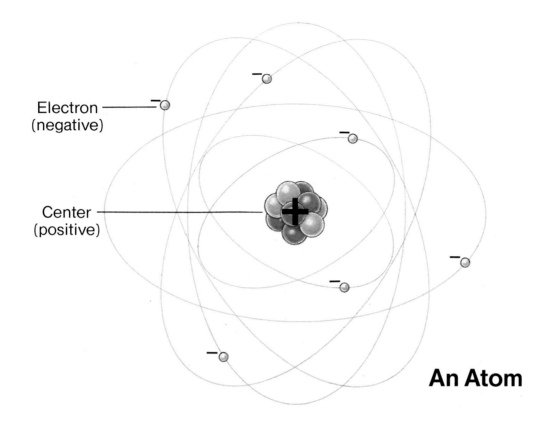

Electron (negative)

Center (positive)

**An Atom**

## What Are Electrons?

Electrons are parts of atoms— the small particles that everything around us is made up of. Water, air, rocks, plants, and animals are all made up of atoms. If you can touch something or weigh it, you can be sure it's made up of atoms! Atoms are so small that a million of them lined up in a row would not be as thick as one strand of your hair.

Electrons move around the centers of atoms. A special kind of attraction keeps the electrons in place. Electrons have a negative (−) charge of electrical energy. The centers of atoms have a positive (+) charge. Negative and positive charges are attracted to each other. The positive center of an atom pulls electrons toward itself, like a magnet pulls pieces of steel.

## What Makes Electrons Move in a Path?

During a thunderstorm, many atoms in the clouds lose some of their electrons. Other atoms gain extra electrons. Most scientists believe it happens in this way:

Water drops form inside a storm cloud. Strong winds hurl the water up toward the top of the cloud. The drops freeze into ice. Some of the ice pieces are small—just tiny slivers. Other pieces become larger and heavier—growing into lumps of hail.

As the pieces of hail get heavier, they start to fall back through the cloud. They crash into rising slivers of ice. During these collisions, some electrons in the ice slivers get pulled away from their atoms. The falling hail picks up these electrons.

The extra electrons give the hail a negative charge. The ice slivers that have lost electrons are left with a positive charge.

Winds carry the light slivers high into the storm cloud, and the tiny pieces of ice give the top part of the cloud a positive charge.

The larger, heavier pieces of hail stay near the bottom of the cloud, and they give the lower part of the cloud a negative charge.

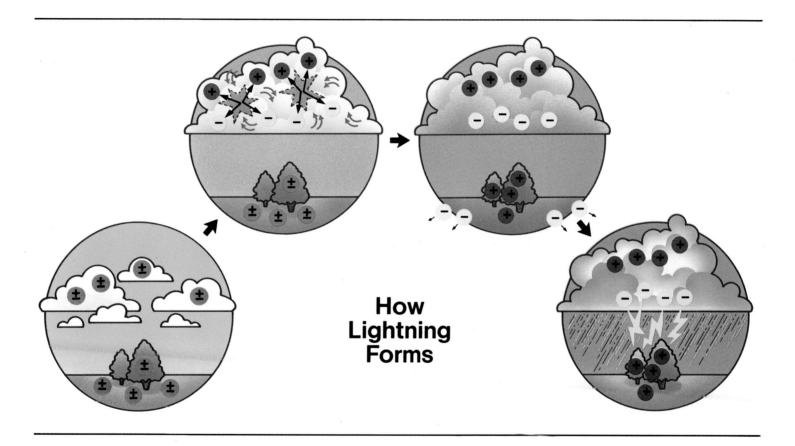

**How Lightning Forms**

The electrons in the bottom of the cloud are attracted to the positive atoms in the top of the cloud. The electrons are also attracted to positive atoms in other clouds and on the ground. If the attraction be-comes strong enough, the electrons may suddenly shoot in a path toward a group of positive atoms. If you are watching the right spot at the right time, you will probably see the lightning flash.

## Where Do the Electrons Go?

Lightning may flash inside a cloud. It can also flash between clouds. Sometimes lightning even shoots sideways out of a cloud into a clear sky.

This unusual photograph captures lightning that started from the ground and shot upward. The lightning bolt traveled from the radio tower up into the storm cloud.

15

The kind of lightning that scientists know the most about, however, is the kind that flashes between clouds and the ground. Lightning that strikes the ground is the easiest to photograph and measure. It also causes the most damage to buildings and living things.

# What Happens during a Lightning Strike?

If you ever see lightning strike nearby, you will never forget the brightness of the light or the loud crack of the thunder. Warren Faidley, the person who took the pictures for this book, was once very close to a lightning strike. He explains it this way:

*About 9:30 P.M. on October 16, 1988, lightning struck a lamp pole just 400 feet in front of me. The strike was so close and so bright I was blinded for a moment. The thunder was immediate—like a million drums going off in my head. I lost my balance. . . . When I got to my feet and closed my eyes, I could still see the outline of the lightning bolt.*

Warren Faidley was lucky. Being anywhere near a lightning strike is *very* dangerous. But no matter how close you are to lightning and how carefully you are watching, you won't be able to see everything that is going on. There are too many things happening too quickly.

Scientists use high-speed cameras, computers, and electronic instruments to study lightning. They create lightning in laboratories, launch rockets into thunderstorms, and examine things that have been struck by lightning. Through their experiments, they have discovered that lightning flashes have different parts, and not all flashes are alike. However, lightning that shoots from a cloud to the ground usually has four main parts: a stepped leader, upward streamers, return strokes, and dart leaders.

Computers are used to record the location of lightning strikes. This information helps experts track the movement of a storm so they can predict areas where lightning may soon strike. In the United States, sensors in 125 locations around the country are hooked up to a national computer network. Within three seconds of a lightning strike near a sensor, the strike shows up on the computers.

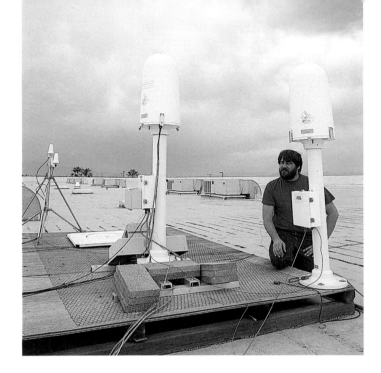

Lightning sensors, such as these, track the electrical charges of lightning strikes. Sensors are important for lightning research, building protection, and forest-fire prevention.

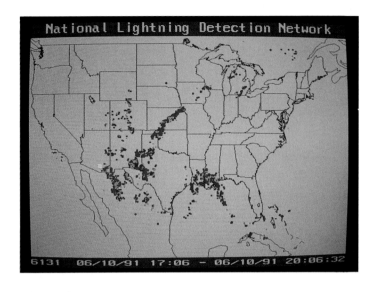

National Lightning Detection Network

6131   06/10/91  17:06  -  06/10/91  20:06:32

To study how lightning works, people can use machines that make lightning-like electrical flashes.

## Stepped Leader

As negative charges collect at the bottom of a storm cloud, a change happens on the ground below. Electrons on the ground "feel" the power of the cloud's negative charges. The electrons are pushed away from the area underneath the cloud. The ground and the objects on it are left with a positive charge.

If you were standing on the ground below a storm cloud, you wouldn't be able to see the electrons move. But you might feel your skin tingle or your hair stand on end.

As the ground becomes positively charged, the attraction between the cloud and the ground grows stronger. Suddenly, electrons shoot down from the cloud. They move in a path that reaches out in different directions—like the branches of a tree. Each branch, or step, is about 50 yards long. This branching path is called a stepped leader.

After the first electrons have blasted their way through the air, other electrons from the cloud follow and make new branches. A stepped leader cuts through the air very quickly. Its average speed is about 75 miles per second—270,000 miles per hour.

## Upward Streamers

As the stepped leader gets close to the ground, electrical sparks rise to meet it. These sparks are called upward streamers. They are paths of positive charge that move up from the ground into the air. Upward streamers are especially likely to shoot up from tall objects, such as trees or buildings.

When the stepped leader meets an upward streamer, a path between the cloud and the earth has been completed. This path is called a lightning channel.

## Return Strokes

As soon as the lightning channel connects the cloud to the earth, electrons in the channel rush into the ground. This movement is called a return stroke.

The electrons move so fast the air around them glows. Most of the light we see during a lightning strike comes from a return stroke.

If you could watch a return stroke in slow motion, you would see that the light from the flash actually starts at the ground and moves upward. The first electrons to pour into the ground are those in the bottom of the lightning channel. That's why the lower end of the channel lights up first. As electrons higher in the channel rush down into the earth, the top part of the channel also begins to glow.

The movement of light up the channel happens too quickly to see. It speeds toward the cloud at 20,000 to 60,000 miles per second. That's fast enough to go all the way around the world once or twice in a single second! To our eyes, the whole path seems to light up at once.

The branches of the stepped leader, however, do not light up as brightly as the

main lightning channel. This is because fewer electrons pass through the branches than through the main channel. Electrons rush out from the stepped leader's branches into the main channel to reach the ground.

After a return stroke, there is a short time when the lightning channel is empty. The electrons that had filled the channel are now in the ground. Some lightning ends after one return stroke. Most lightning strikes, however, have three or four return strokes.

## Dart Leaders

Once the lightning channel is empty, electrons from another part of the cloud may rush down into it. This movement of new electrons into the main channel is called a dart leader.

After the electrons have moved into the channel, another return stroke happens. Then another dart leader. And another return stroke. A single lightning channel can be used by several dart leaders and return strokes.

When you see lightning that flickers, you are really seeing the light from the different return strokes. The flashes are happening so quickly you cannot tell them apart. The return strokes just look like one flickering flash.

To catch the separate movements of the dart leaders and their return strokes, Warren Faidley moved his camera as he shot these photographs.

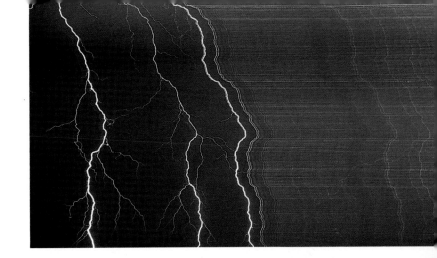

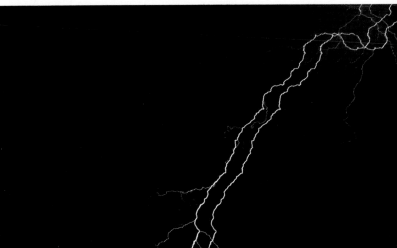

# What Happens When Lightning Strikes the Ground

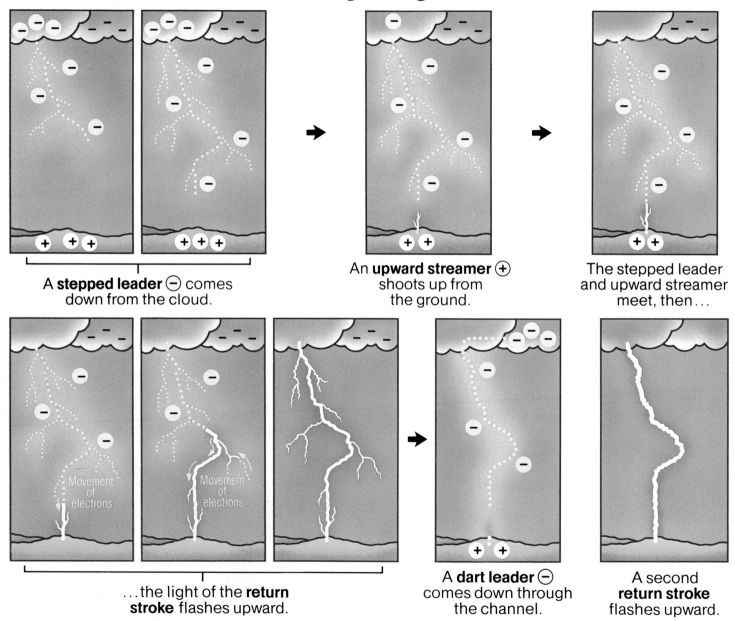

A **stepped leader** ⊖ comes down from the cloud.

An **upward streamer** ⊕ shoots up from the ground.

The stepped leader and upward streamer meet, then...

...the light of the **return stroke** flashes upward.

A **dart leader** ⊖ comes down through the channel.

A second **return stroke** flashes upward.

Movement of electrons

Movement of electrons

26

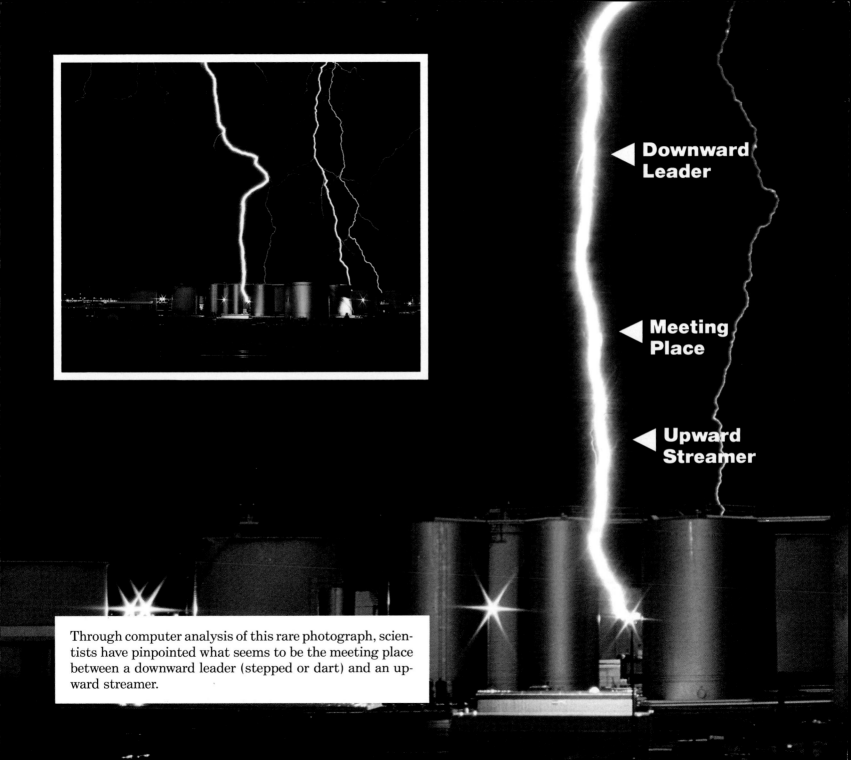

Downward
Leader ◄

Meeting
Place ◄

Upward
Streamer ◄

Through computer analysis of this rare photograph, scientists have pinpointed what seems to be the meeting place between a downward leader (stepped or dart) and an upward streamer.

# How Long and How Wide Is Lightning?

The average length of lightning that flashes between a cloud and the ground is about 3 or 4 miles. But lightning can be much shorter or longer. Sparks of lightning only a few yards long can sometimes be seen in clouds. On the other hand, a bolt of lightning was once measured that shot sideways through the air for more than 90 miles.

Although lightning is often several miles long, it is not very wide. The average lightning channel is only about an inch across.

## What Is Thunder?

Thunder is the noise made by lightning. During a return stroke, the lightning channel becomes very hot. In fact, the temperature of the channel as electrons pass through it is about five times as hot as the sun.

The air around the lightning channel heats up instantly. Since air takes up more space when it is hot, the air around the channel explodes outward in all directions. The explosion sends out waves that are heard as sound—the sound of thunder.

Light travels much faster than sound. When lightning strikes one mile away, you see the flash almost instantly. But the thunder takes about 5 seconds to reach you.

If you want to know how far away a lightning flash was, count the seconds between the light and the first sound of thunder. For every 5 seconds you count, the lightning flash was 1 mile away. If you count 20 seconds, the lightning was 4 miles away. If you count only 10 seconds, you'd better take cover fast! The lightning was only 2 miles away.

If you see a flash of lightning but don't hear the thunder, the lightning was probably too far away to hear. You usually can't hear thunder that happens 15 or more miles away.

Since lightning can be several miles long, the thunder from different parts of a lightning channel reaches your ears at different times. This is what makes thunder rumble and roll. Echoes of thunder bouncing off mountains can also cause rumbling.

# What Kind of a Cloud Makes Lightning?

Lightning can happen during snowstorms, hailstorms, sandstorms, and tornadoes. Lightning may flash in the dust and ash of erupting volcanoes. Once in a while, lightning even seems to explode out of clear blue skies. But most lightning, by far, comes from large clouds called thunderheads.

Lightning can shoot out of the sides of funnel clouds. This photograph was taken from a video tape on tornadoes.

30

## Thunderheads

Thunderheads are the towering clouds you see during thunderstorms. In addition to lightning, these giant clouds can bring rain, sleet, hail, snow, and strong winds. Another name for a thunderhead is a cumulonimbus (kyu-mya-lo-NIM-buhs) cloud.

Thunderheads usually form on warm, sunny days. The sun heats moist air near the ground. As the air gets warm, it rises. White, puffy clouds start to appear in the sky. These clouds are called cumulus (KYU-mya-les) clouds.

Sometimes a few cumulus clouds join together. More warm air rises from the ground. The clouds grow larger and larger. A new cloud begins to take shape. The growing cloud sucks in more warm air. The air rushes up through the center of the cloud, like smoke up a chimney.

These three photos were taken 10 minutes apart. They show a growing group of cumulus clouds.

32

Eventually the top of the cloud hits cold air. Drops of water and bits of ice form. The cloud darkens. Pieces of ice grow into large balls of hail. The cloud is now a thunderhead.

As long as there are no strong winds blowing from the side, the thunderhead will keep growing. Some cumulonimbus clouds grow to over 10 miles in height.

Strong winds blow through the thunderhead. Hail and ice slivers collide. Soon there are flashes of lightning.

A single thunderhead can cause a storm with lightning. But a thunderhead doesn't last long. The average cumulonimbus cloud starts to take shape, grows into a towering giant, and disappears—all in about one hour. It produces only 15 to 30 minutes of lightning and thunder.

Yet many thunderstorms last longer than 30 minutes. As one thunderhead disappears, another grows next to it. A storm with an hour of lightning is usually made of two or three different thunderheads. From the ground, though, you may not be able to tell how many thunderheads are in the storm.

# Where Does Lightning Happen?

Lightning strikes some parts of the earth more than others. There are few lightning strikes near the north or south poles. The weather near the poles is usually not warm or moist enough to create thunderheads. These areas have a thunderstorm only once every 10 years or so.

Thunderstorms *are* common in many areas near the equator. The air in the tropics has lots of the warmth and moisture needed to form a thunderhead. In places such as Panama and Indonesia, thunder is heard about 200 days per year.

The amount of lightning in an area is sometimes measured by counting "thunderstorm days." A thunderstorm day is a day on which thunder can be heard—no matter whether thunder is heard once or a hundred times. Counting thunderstorm days can't tell you exactly how often lightning strikes an area. But it can give scientists a way to compare the amount of lightning in different places.

People who live in Kampala, Uganda, hear thunder about 240 days per year. In comparison, New York City has about 31 thunderstorm days a year. Paris and Rome have about 21, and London has about 16.

In the United States and Canada, the area with the most thunderstorm days is the southwest coast of Florida—with about 90 thunderstorm days per year.

# The Average Number of Thunderstorm Days in a Year

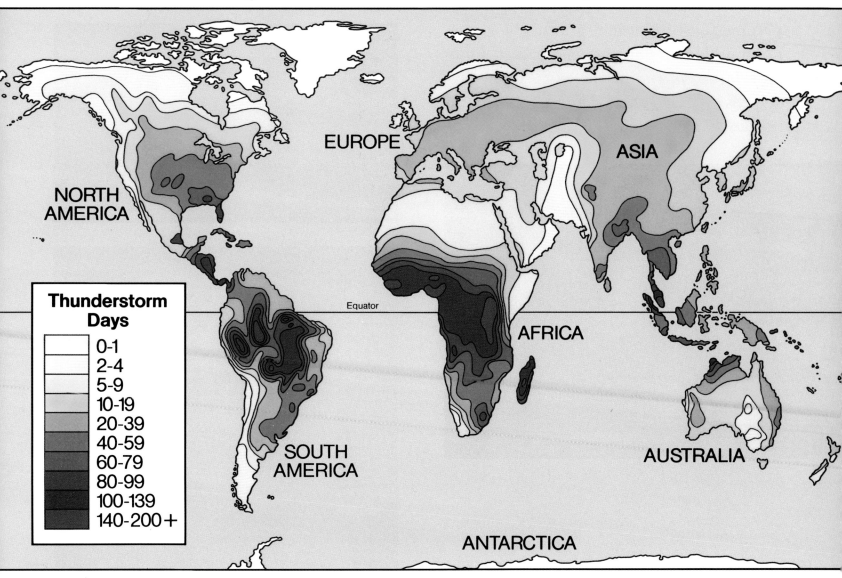

**Thunderstorm Days**

- 0-1
- 2-4
- 5-9
- 10-19
- 20-39
- 40-59
- 60-79
- 80-99
- 100-139
- 140-200+

NORTH AMERICA

EUROPE

ASIA

AFRICA

SOUTH AMERICA

AUSTRALIA

ANTARCTICA

Equator

# Different Kinds of Lightning

Sometimes lightning is a bright streak in a black night. Other times it lights up a large section of the sky. Lightning may even be ball-shaped and float through the air or roll around on the ground.

## HEAT LIGHTNING
Flashes that light up distant clouds are often called heat lightning. The lightning is too far away to see a streak or hear any thunder. Heat lightning probably got its name because it is often seen on hot summer nights.

## RIBBON LIGHTNING

When lightning looks like a blurred streak with more than one flash in it, the lightning is called ribbon lightning. Ribbon lightning happens when a lightning channel cuts through strong winds. The winds push the channel sideways, so the lightning looks wider than usual, and the separate return strokes can be seen.

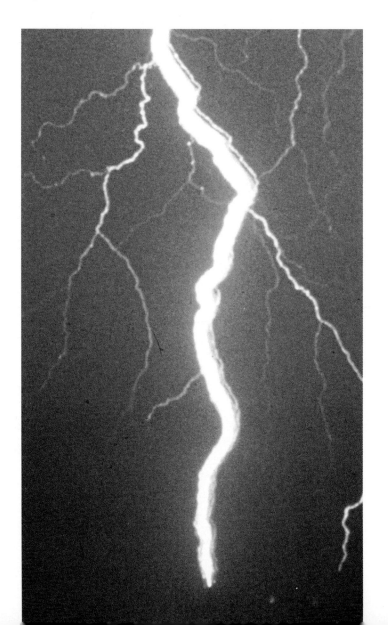

## BEAD AND ROCKET LIGHTNING

Some kinds of lightning play tricks on our eyes as they flash across the sky. It is almost impossible to photograph these kinds of lightning because the illusions are due to timing. In bead lightning, parts of the lightning channel seem to stay lit longer than others. As the channel fades, it looks like a string of beads. In rocket lightning, one section of the flash lights up at a time as the lightning crosses the sky. This photograph shows lightning that appeared to be rocket lightning.

## BALL LIGHTNING

Balls of light, called ball lightning, are sometimes seen near lightning strikes. Ball lightning usually looks about the size of an apple or a grapefruit. It has been seen near the ground or falling from clouds. Sometimes ball lightning even appears inside buildings. People have reported seeing ball lightning float through the air, hang motionless above the ground, or roll along a road.

Most ball lightning lasts only a few seconds. Although it has been seen in a variety of colors, the most common colors seem to be orange, red, and yellow. Sometimes ball lightning disappears with a loud explosion. At other times, it just fades quietly into the air.

41

## Safety in a Thunderstorm

Lightning strikes are a major cause of forest fires. These natural fires can play an important role in keeping forests healthy. But forestry experts must keep a close eye on them so they don't grow out of control.

There are many kinds of lightning, and they are all dangerous.

Each year, an average of 150 to 200 people are killed by lightning in just the United States. Even more people are injured by being so close to a lightning strike that some of the electricity goes through them. That is why it is very important to take shelter indoors whenever you see a thunderstorm approaching. Don't wait for the rain to start or the thunder to get close. If you can't reach a building, the inside of a car with closed windows is another safe spot.

Once you have found shelter, you need not be afraid. It is very unlikely the place you are in would ever be struck by lightning. But just to be safe, have an adult unplug any TVs, stereos, and computers before the storm begins. After the storm starts, use the telephone *only* for emergencies. Stay away from metal objects such as faucet handles and screen doors. Wait until the storm is over to do dishes or take a bath.

If you are ever caught outside during a thunderstorm, here are some things to remember:

*If you are swimming or boating, get out of the water immediately.* Lightning travels easily through water. You can be injured or killed if lightning strikes the water or the land nearby.

*If you cannot get to shelter, make sure you are not the highest object in the area.* Lightning often strikes tall objects, especially if they stand alone in open areas. Hurry off the tops of hills, and get out of open, flat fields. Crouch down in the lowest spot you can find. Keep away from metal objects such as bicycles, golf clubs, tractors, and wire fences. Take off shoes with metal cleats. If you are in a group in an open area, spread out—with several yards between each person.

*Do not stand under a tall tree or any other towering object.* If you are in an area with lots of trees, look for shelter underneath a group of trees that are all about the same height. Stand away from the trunks and roots. (When you are camping, be sure to choose a safe place to pitch your tent.)

*If you feel your skin tingle or your hair stand on end, lightning may be about to strike.* Crouch down and bend over your knees right away. Do not *lie* down.

Many cattle, sheep, and other animals that graze in open fields are killed each year by lightning.

On a warm summer evening, thunderheads rumble overhead. Bright lights flash in the darkness. Long trails of light streak through the air. Long ago, mysterious sights like these could only be explained by magic.

Each year, scientists learn more about lightning. But there are still many unanswered questions. Exactly what happens during each part of a lightning flash? Can we predict when and where lightning will strike? What is ball lightning, and how does it form?

When we see lightning blaze a jagged path through a storm, we have some understanding of the powerful forces at work inside a thunderhead. But we are also reminded that some of lightning's mysteries have yet to be explained.

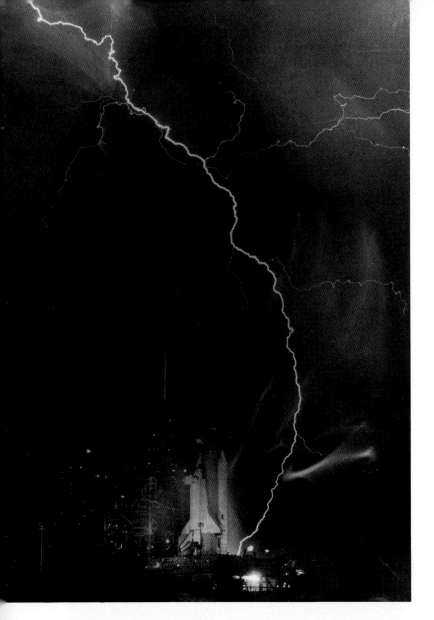

Lightning can harm rockets and space shuttles. On August 30, 1983, this lightning bolt just missed hitting a space shuttle ready for takeoff at the John F. Kennedy Space Center. In March 1987, lightning struck a remote-controlled space rocket, and it broke apart in midair.

## Fascinating Facts

*The Greeks believed that places struck by lightning were sacred. They often built temples to Zeus on sites that had been hit by lightning.*

*Stories about lightning from southern Africa tell about a giant bird called Umpundulo. As Umpundulo dives from the clouds to the earth, lightning flashes from the bird's bright feathers. Thunder is the sound of the great bird's beating wings.*

*Lightning hits large airplanes about once every 5,000 to 10,000 hours of flying time. A plane flying 12 hours a day will be hit about once every two years. Usually the plane can keep flying. In 1964, a plane circling the Chicago airport was hit by lightning five times in 20 minutes.*

*About 156 billion, billion electrons flow down into the ground during a typical lightning strike.*

*by lightning an average of 23 times a year. During one thunderstorm, it was struck 8 times in 24 minutes.*

*Earth isn't the only planet where lightning happens. TV cameras on the spacecrafts* Voyager I *and* II *showed lightning flashes around Jupiter. Lightning is also thought to happen on Saturn, Uranus, Neptune, and Venus.*

A lightning flash is hot enough to melt sand. When lightning strikes sand, it leaves behind a glasslike tube called a fulgurite. Some fulgurites are more than eight feet long and are branched like the roots of a tree. This fulgurite was found in the dirt of an Arizona desert after a July storm.

*When lightning flashes, it heats up gases in the air. Some of these gases mix with the rain and fall to the ground as natural fertilizer. Another gas, called ozone, rises into the atmosphere. This gas helps protect the earth from the sun's harmful rays.*

*Lightning* does *strike the same place twice—or even many times. The Empire State Building in New York City is struck*

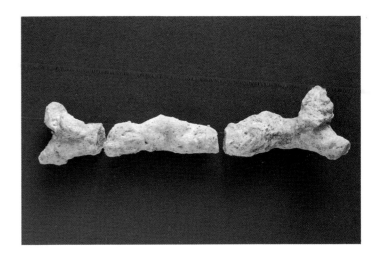

# Glossary

**Atoms:** The tiny particles everything is made up of. If atoms lose any of their electrons, they have a positive (+) electrical charge.

**Cumulonimbus clouds:** The towering clouds that cause thunderstorms. Cumulonimbus clouds are also called thunderheads.

**Cumulus clouds:** The white, puffy clouds that are common on hot summer days. Cumulus clouds sometimes join together, forming thunderheads.

**Dart leader:** The movement of electrons out of a thunderhead into a lightning channel that has already been formed

**Electricity:** The movement of electrons or positive atoms from one place to another

**Electrons:** The tiny parts of atoms that rush through the air during a lightning strike. Electrons have a negative (−) electrical charge.

**Fulgurite:** A tube of melted sand made by lightning striking the sand

**Lightning:** A large electrical spark created when electrons move suddenly through the air

**Lightning channel:** The path electrons take through the air

**Negative (−) charge:** One of the two kinds of electrical charges. This charge is strongly attracted to things that have a positive (+) charge. Electrons have a negative (−) charge.

**Positive (+) charge:** One of the two kinds of electrical charges. This charge is strongly attracted to things that have a negative (−) charge. Atoms have a positive (+) charge after they lose electrons.

**Return stroke:** The part of lightning that gives off the most light. In most lightning strikes, a return stroke is the movement of electrons from the lightning channel into the ground.

**Stepped leader:** The crooked, forked path electrons take before a lightning channel has been formed

**Thunder:** The sound made by the heated air that expands around a lightning channel

**Thunderheads:** The towering clouds that often cause thunderstorms. Thunderheads are also called cumulonimbus clouds.

**Upward streamers:** Electrical sparks that move upward from the ground as a stepped leader shoots down from a cloud